MEN IN BLACK

KENNY ABDO

Fly!
An Imprint of Abdo Zoom
abdobooks.com

abdobooks.com

Published by Abdo Zoom, a division of ABDO, P.O. Box 398166, Minneapolis, Minnesota 55439. Copyright © 2020 by Abdo Consulting Group, Inc. International copyrights reserved in all countries. No part of this book may be reproduced in any form without written permission from the publisher. Fly!™ is a trademark and logo of Abdo Zoom.

Printed in the United States of America, North Mankato, Minnesota.
102019
012020

Photo Credits: Alamy, AP Images, Everett Collection, iStock, Shutterstock, ©Planetkazik p15 / CC BY-SA 4.0
Production Contributors: Kenny Abdo, Jennie Forsberg, Grace Hansen
Design Contributors: Dorothy Toth, Neil Klinepier, Pakou Moua

Library of Congress Control Number: 2019941599

Publisher's Cataloging-in-Publication Data

Names: Abdo, Kenny, author.
Title: Men in black / by Kenny Abdo
Description: Minneapolis, Minnesota : Abdo Zoom, 2020 | Series: Guidebooks to the unexplained | Includes online resources and index.
Identifiers: ISBN 9781532129360 (lib. bdg.) | ISBN 9781644942895 (pbk.) | ISBN 9781098220341 (ebook) | ISBN 9781098220839 (Read-to-Me ebook)
Subjects: LCSH: Men in black (UFO phenomenon)--Juvenile literature. | Extraterrestrial beings--Juvenile literature. | Conspiracy--Juvenile literature. | Legends--Juvenile literature. | UFOs--Juvenile literature.
Classification: DDC 001.942--dc23

TABLE OF CONTENTS

MEN IN BLACK

No matter how, where, or when—
if you have an alien encounter,
chances are you will be confronted
by the Men in Black (MIB).

5

The idea of the MIB has grown into a key fixation for **UFO** investigators and has spread deep into popular culture.

CLASSIFICATION

Always wearing black suits with dark sunglasses, the MIB usually arrive in groups of two or three.

Some have described the MIB as having strange appearances. Some said the MIB were aliens trying to cover-up their own existence.

Whoever they are, the MIB have only one mission—to silence those who witness the strange and paranormal.

DECLASSIFIED

A pilot named Kenneth Arnold had his own **UFO** glimpse in 1947. It is considered the first widely reported sighting. It was soon dismissed by unknown US government agents as a **mirage**.

Harold Dahl was on a trip in 1947. He noticed six flying objects hovering above his boat. After reporting it, he was visited by a man in black. The stranger insisted that Dahl forget about what he saw.

Dr. Albert Bender started the International Flying Saucer Bureau (IFSB). In 1955, he wrote a paper that proved the US Government covered up **UFOs**. Three MIB visited his home. They warned him not to release the paper. Bender immediately shut down the IFSB.

Danny Gordon was a radio host who snapped photos of **UFOs**. He was interviewed by two MIB who claimed to work for a magazine. When they left, Gordon found his UFO photos mysteriously missing from his office.

Paul Miller reported seeing a bright disc in the sky after a hunting trip. After, he was approached by three MIB at work. They suggested he keep quiet about what he saw. Miller recalled, "They seemed to know everything about me. Where I worked, my name, everything."

Actor Dan Aykroyd claims his **paranormal** TV show was shut down by the MIB. When he stepped outside of the **studio**, he noticed a tall man in black across the street staring at him. Aykroyd learned the show was suddenly cancelled when he returned.

19

IN MEDIA

Aside from appearing in graphic novels and comic books, the MIB have major Hollywood status. There have been four Men in Black movies in a monstrously popular franchise.

If you **encounter** an alien, it'd be best to keep it to yourself. Anything is better than a knock on the door from the men in black.

GLOSSARY

encounter – unexpectedly faced with something difficult or hostile.

franchise – a collection of related movies in a series.

mirage – something that appears to be real but is not.

paranormal – an occurrence beyond the scope of scientific understanding.

studio – an artificial setting where a movie or television program is filmed.

UFO – a mysterious object seen in the sky that has no explanation. UFO is short for Unidentified Flying Object.

ONLINE RESOURCES

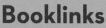

Booklinks
NONFICTION NETWORK
FREE! ONLINE NONFICTION RESOURCES

To learn more about men in black, please visit abdobooklinks.com or scan this QR code. These links are routinely monitored and updated to provide the most current information available.

INDEX